Philosophical Thinking is Yoga for the Mind©

Upper West Side Philosophers, Inc. provides a publication venue for original philosophical thinking steeped in lived life, in line with our motto: *philosophical living & lived philosophy*.

A weak person isn't necessarily a burden on others. Each of us freely disposes of his or her own weakness, and it's up to us to employ it judiciously.
—Alexandre Jollien

Alexandre Jollien, who is the first and only philosopher and spiritual teacher in history to have been born with cerebral palsy, tells the story of how he grew up in an institution for the severely disabled and was destined to roll cigars; how he discovered philosophy, which changed his life forever, helping him to confront his fate, endow it with meaning, and turn his disability into a source of strength and creative energy; how, against all odds, he fought his way out of the institution and into high school and university, where as an undergraduate he wrote *In Praise of Weakness* …

Imbued with human warmth and wisdom, this modern Socratic dialogue is a poignant testament to the inestimable value of friendship, the power of imagination, and the will to overcome.

ALSO BY ALEXANDRE JOLLIEN

• *Le métier d'homme*
(The Craft of Being Human)

• *Petit traité de l'abandon: Pensées pour accueillir
la vie telle qu'elle se propose*
*(A Short Treatise on Surrender: Thoughts on
Welcoming Life as It Is)*

• *Le philosophe nu*
(The Naked Philosopher)

• *La construction de soi: Un usage de la philosophie*
(The Construction of Self: Uses of Philosophy)

• *Vivre sans pourquoi: Itinéraire spirituel
d'un philosophe en Corée*
*(Living without Why: The Spiritual Itinerary
of a Philosopher in Korea)*

In Praise of Weakness

Alexandre Jollien

With a Foreword by Matthieu Ricard

Translated from the French
by Michael Eskin

Upper West Side Philosophers, Inc. • New York

Published by Upper West Side Philosophers, Inc.
P. O. Box 250645, New York, NY 10025, USA
www.westside-philosophers.com

A UWSP SOFTCOVER ORIGINAL

Cover: UWSP, based on a design by Michael Wörgötter

Yoga for the Mind©

Cataloging-in-Publication Data

Names: Jollien, Alexandre, 1975- author.
Title: In praise of weakness / Alexandre Jollien ; with a foreword by
   Matthieu Ricard ; translated from the French by Michael Eskin.
Other titles: Eloge de la faiblesse. English
Description: New York : Upper West Side Philosophers, Inc., 2017.
   | Series: Subway line ; No. 12
Identifiers: LCCN 2017000450 (print) | LCCN 2017010058(ebook) |
   ISBN 9781935830429 (alk. paper) | ISBN 9781935830436
Subjects: LCSH: Jollien, Alexandre, 1975- |
   Philosophy--Switzerland--Biography. | Cerebral palsied--
   Biography. | Developmental disabilities--Patients--Biography. |
   People with disabilities--Biography.
Classification: LCC B4651.J654 A3 2017 (ebook) | LCC B4651.J654
   (print) | DDC 199/.494--dc23
LC record available at https://lccn.loc.gov/2017010058

With the support of the Swiss
Arts Council Pro Helvetia.

swiss arts council
prohelvetia

*For my parents
and
for Étienne Parrat for the spirit of
her faithful friendship.*

*This book also owes a great debt to
Pierre Carruzzo, André Gilloz, Antoine Maillard and
Georges Savoy, whose support allowed me to embark
on the liberating path of higher education. And for
Laure, Marie-Madelaine, Nicole, Henri and Willy,
who, together with them and many others, have
accompanied me on my life's joyous, if at times
chaotic, journey.*

*All my gratitude, finally, to my childhood
companions, who have given me so much.*

contents

"I have all the time in the world!" Socrates says to Alexandre Jollien in this wonderful book.

Who wouldn't love to open their heart to Socrates and be guided by him through an intimate introspective dialogue? Alexandre used this approach during the most trying times of his life, as he badly needed a benevolent mentor. A mentor who would be available anywhere, anytime; a trustworthy guide whom he could rely upon on his arduous journey. Someone who would extend a loving hand in times of sadness and give him an energetic push in times of discouragement.

Alexandre is the first great philosopher in history who has suffered from a serious congenital disorder. To me, he is a dear friend and a most remarkable human being.

Disabled since birth, he spent seventeen years with little contact with the outside world in a center for children with cerebral palsy. There, he and his companions huddled close together to find some solace in the midst of their caregivers' lack of understanding. As he recounts in this book:

> The present was … the sole focus of all our
> preoccupations, all our thoughts … Mutual
> gestures of friendship helped us through diffi-
> cult moments and prevented us from becom-
> ing discouraged. Friendship united us, made
> us stronger. We loved each other. That's how it
> was. We didn't have a choice. The tenderness
> of our mutual affection alleviated our loneli-
> ness. Collaboration was absolutely vital if we
> wanted to attain our main goal: making
> progress … life lay before us—open-ended
> and rife with possibility—and we had every-
> thing to gain.

He was able to move on from this dire situation to become a compelling thinker who has
inspired thousands of people through his raw
authenticity and depth of thought. Soothed by
the gentle presence of his comrades and by the
kindness occasionally shown by others, Alexandre's disability—or "weakness," as he calls it—
became the fertile ground for his admirable
intellectual and spiritual accomplishments.

Alexandre's disability is very obvious and
often attracts cruel remarks from insensitive
passers-by. It confronts us with our own image,
our conceit, of being 'normal'. Let's be honest:
we are all afflicted with handicaps that might
be less obvious and more easily concealed, but

nonetheless crippling. They manifest as the various dysfunctions of our minds, clouded by confusion, scorched by animosity, poisoned by jealousy, shrunk by selfishness, distorted by pride, and torn apart by obsessive desires. Becoming aware of our own shortcomings is a good lesson in humility.

Thanks to travelling through his inner world in the company of Socrates, Alexandre, a lovable person facing adverse circumstances, discovered his inner richness. He became fully aware that no one should remain imprisoned within conventional norms, since the beauty of being human is to free oneself from the shackles of such conventions.

Recently, one of his daughters (he has three children) told him, "Papa, we love you." Alexandre asked his children in turn: "If you had had to choose between a handicapped and a normal father, which one would you have taken?" They answered that none of them would have ever dreamed of exchanging him for a "normal" father.

Alexandre never tries to hide his disability. One of his classmates in the public school he eventually was sent to had a misshapen thumb and always kept his hand in his pocket. Alexandre told him: "Don't try to hide your disability.

Look at me, I would have to walk around wrapped in a garbage bag!" He realized that attempting to hide one's disability leads to isolation and estrangement. He had to come to terms with it. "To achieve this," adds Alexandre, "knowing one's weaknesses is key."

Times of intense suffering allowed Alexandre to open his eyes and reach toward others. "It is they who saved me," he says. "I feel the opposite of what Sartre wrote ('Hell is other people'). I would rather say: 'Salvation is other people'."

Anyone who meets Alexandre quickly finds him to be a very endearing person. His candor and his sense of humor transform his "weakness" into the strength to spark friendships and gently invite other people into his sphere. There, they rediscover the potential for kindness that we all have within ourselves.

Alexandre cannot use his hands to write, but his books have been able to touch the hearts of hundreds of thousands of readers all over the world. His words surge not only from his brilliant mind, but also from his heart and guts.

I am, therefore, delighted that *In Praise of Weakness* is finally available to English readers.

Matthieu Ricard

In Praise of Weakness

The characters in this book speak under fictive names—with the exception of Father Morand … and Socrates.

> *It is through wonder that men now begin and*
> *originally began to philosophize ... He who won-*
> *ders and is perplexed feels that he is ignorant ...*
> *It was to escape ignorance, therefore, that men*
> *studied philosophy.*
>
> —*Aristotle*

And so philosophy was born of man's wonder at the world. Going beyond what 'goes without saying' and the clichés of everyday life—that's what distinguishes the philosopher.

From the beginning, philosophers have been preoccupied with questions that may have seemed self-evident, if not trivial, to their contemporaries. In the following pages, I endeavor to apply this method to the experience of growing up in a residential care facility: disabled since birth, I spent seventeen years in a center for children with cerebral palsy.

"Memory is the stomach of the mind," writes St. Augustine. This creative process led me to ruminate on some of the experiences along my journey, turning my past into pasture for my

reflections. Having settled on the menu, I still
had to find the appropriate digestif. Why not
the tonic of humor—that royal road to putting
in perspective life's often tragic situations? "If
you want to know who the good philosopher is,
line them all up," Nietzsche suggests. "The one
who laughs is the good one."

I cannot write by hand. Therefore, I had to
dictate these pages into a computer that tran-
scribed them—which is why the style sometimes feels like spoken language.

As to my choice of the Socratic dialogue, it
faithfully reflects the manner in which I learned
to philosophize. In order to overcome the obstacles of daily life, I read the philosophers. They
became my favorite interlocutors. Among them,
Socrates played a decisive role: my nascent interest in philosophy coincided with my discov-
ery of his thinking. Also, it seems to me that the
complete absence of prejudice that we com-
monly associate with Socrates made him an
ideal traveling companion for the adventure
that I am about to relate.

Where did this strange dialogue take place? Feel free to take your pick! In Greece, perhaps, amid the bustling crowds of anonymous passers-by in the agora: some heading to the market or visiting an old friend, others returning home from the doctor's or on their way there … Or was it, more modestly, in the poorly-lit dormitory where under the secret cover of night I lay awake surrounded by my brothers-in-misfortune? When? No one knows. Why? Search well and you shall find. There is meaning in everything.

The conversations with Socrates were frequent and went on for a long time. Here, I only relate their gist, sparing the reader the long hours of discussion during which Socrates confounded his interlocutor, unmasked his most egregious prejudices, and forced him to clearly define each of the key concepts used.

ALEXANDRE: Socrates?

SOCRATES: Indeed, I am.

ALEXANDRE: Greetings, Socrates!

SOCRATES: Greetings? What is it that you want?

ALEXANDRE: To tell you … how extremely grateful I am.

SOCRATES: What for? What have I done for you?

ALEXANDRE: You have given me the greatest of gifts!

SOCRATES: Have we met before?

ALEXANDRE: In a certain sense.

SOCRATES: Now you are making me curious.

ALEXANDRE: If you are not in too much of a hurry …

SOCRATES: I have all the time in the world! Go ahead … unless, that is, you don't like talking.

ALEXANDRE: Well, then, allow me to introduce myself: my name is Alexandre. I am twenty-three years old, and I am majoring in philosophy at the university.

SOCRATES: So far, nothing out of the ordinary.

ALEXANDRE: Still …

SOCRATES: Back to your story, then. Proceed with confidence!

ALEXANDRE: As I said, I am twenty-three, and I have embarked on the study of philosophy.

SOCRATES: Go on, step by step. Tell me everything. Stick to the facts and try not to digress. If need be, I will ask the necessary questions. First, tell me about your childhood.

ALEXANDRE: Where to begin? I saw the light of day on November 26, 1975, in a little Swiss village that I had to leave almost immediately. A birth accident wrested me from my family, forcing my parents to put me in a specialized institution— 'would-be specialized' is probably more accurate. There, I had …

SOCRATES: Let's not get ahead of ourselves! What birth accident?

ALEXANDRE: Athetosis.

SOCRATES: Can you be more specific!

ALEXANDRE: As you can see, I have great difficulty controlling my movements, my gait is unsteady, and I speak slowly. These are the long-term effects of a particular form of asphyxiation that goes by the scientific name of 'athetosis'.

SOCRATES: And what was the cause of it?

ALEXANDRE: Turning one too many somersaults

in my mother's womb, I got my neck all tangled up in the umbilical cord … You are looking at the fallout now.

My birth transpired in a frenzied atmosphere. My mother told me that what she saw emerging from her womb was a baby that was completely black and did not cry. "Is he dead?" she screamed. "No," the midwife replied, "but we don't know if he'll make it." For a brief moment, the baby fixed its mother's tired gaze, and then they were separated. I was taken to a hospital where I received cardiopulmonary resuscitation.

SOCRATES: Your last chance?

ALEXANDRE: More like my first and only chance! To my mother, the word 'resuscitation' meant hope. Deprived of her newborn, she stubbornly insisted with the attending medical staff: "He must live, he must live, no matter how—so long as he lives!" As fate would have it, her wish was granted. Ten days later, she was holding a magnificent baby in her arms. The doctors abstained from making any prognoses about the infant's development. But that didn't matter; her child was alive.

the strange creature that I am

ALEXANDRE: Since I was four, I have undergone multiple therapies: physical therapy, ergotherapy, speech therapy … All that to fix the strange creature that I am.

SOCRATES: Strange?

ALEXANDRE: My good Socrates, I was so different: I couldn't walk at all. I expressed myself awkwardly. And my motor skills left a lot to be desired in terms of control and precision, to say the least. In sum, I really wasn't normal.

SOCRATES: So, what did you do?

ALEXANDRE: A myriad of exercises: I practiced sitting straight, coordinating my arms and legs, controlling my jerky movements. I learned how to use knife and fork (without slitting my neighbor's throat). And it wasn't long before I became an expert at wielding the soup spoon (or was it the dessert spoon?). Then there were also my daily attempts at beating my own record in one thousand meters on all fours …

SOCRATES: I imagine that all of these excellent practical results took a lot of time and hard work on your part.

ALEXANDRE: At the Center, there was no short-age of activities. Classes were often interrupted by therapeutic exercises. My friend Luc, for instance, spent long hours learning to articulate tedious sounds. He was in constant and merci-less battle with words like 'tone', 'cone', 'bone', 'roam', 'wound', 'round'. No one could have been more stubbornly persistent.

Moreover, like all children, we too had to follow the regular school curriculum, which included learning the alphabet, multiplication … In short, more than enough to fill our days.

SOCRATES: Be more specific! How did you spend your …

ALEXANDRE: We would typically get back to the Center on Sunday night, around 7pm, all clean and neatly dressed, the pain of parting from our families still etched in our dejected faces. The consolations of nightfall would gradually return us to our regular state of mind. In the morning, full of energy, we would leave our dorm rooms, go down to the first floor, and the day could begin. Throughout the year, we had plenty of activities: therapies, treatments, school, recreation—such was our daily routine. In the evening, we would go back up to the second floor and get ready for bed. Lights out was at 8pm. Monday, Tuesday, Wednesday, Thursday and Friday unfolded in rhythmic succession; though never completely alike, the days rolled on with astonishing regularity. Ineluctably, we were carried along by time's onward flow without ever so much as asking why.

SOCRATES: And what about your interaction with the world outside?

ALEXANDRE: That happened only on rare occasions. My companions and I spent most of our time at the Center, where we were looked after by maids, a cook, a doctor, a dentist and a psychologist. This was my world: a group of unique characters outside the norm.

SOCRATES: You have invoked the notions of 'norm' and 'normality'. Could you give me a precise definition of 'normal'?

ALEXANDRE: A precise definition? Let me try: 'normal' is whatever conforms to the majority or the average of cases or customs; whatever is common, familiar. For instance, it seems to me that it is normal for a twelve-year old to be able to walk, talk, read and write …

SOCRATES: That's how you would define it?

ALEXANDRE: In general terms, yes.

SOCRATES: Go on, then!

ALEXANDRE: At the Center, nothing could be taken for granted. Everything was a source of wonder for us. Each day held infinite surprises, both good and bad. Boredom was not an option. We had our sights set on one thing only, one single goal: making progress. Everything else—whether the food was good or bad, whether others did better in school—was secondary.

SOCRATES: Didn't you think about the future?

ALEXANDRE: There are priorities, and there are less important matters. Making progress, getting healthier and stronger, was our top priority. Every second of every minute had to be devoted to getting closer to this goal. No 'tomorrow' or 'later' for us. The future was limited to weekends, when we'd go home to our families. That, to me, was the essence of happiness: spending two days with my mother and father, and my brother Franck!

SOCRATES: Is it a good thing when the present claims all your attention?

ALEXANDRE: I don't know … The force of circumstance had made us natural-born realists by default, so to speak—we were always immersed in the present, in the concrete here and now. As for the past, it barely had any significance for us. Whether you were in first or second grade mattered little. The present was, as you put it, the sole focus of all our preoccupations, all our thoughts. We didn't unnecessarily complicate things.

ALEXANDRE: Our daily life was marked by a similar simplicity: we loved each other in a simple, unadorned way. Attachments were formed naturally, reinforced by the peculiarity of our condition, by the singular reality of our community. Mutual gestures of friendship helped us through difficult moments and prevented us from becoming discouraged. Friendship united us, made us stronger. We loved each other. That's how it was. We didn't have a choice. The tenderness of our mutual affection alleviated our loneliness.

SOCRATES: If I understand you correctly, the spontaneity of your relationships was in a certain sense born of shared suffering. You were all pursuing the same goal.

ALEXANDRE: Collaboration was absolutely vital if we wanted to achieve our main goal: making progress, continuing to develop, becoming more and more like the other children, the 'normal' ones. This dominated all our endeavors and gave meaning to everything else. Our entire existence could be summed up as follows:

life lay before us—open-ended and rife with possibility—and we had everything to gain. Our only task consisted in doing everything in our power to make it happen, to make progress and grow.

SOCRATES: I have to admit that I find it hard to conceive where you drew your strength from.

ALEXANDRE: I don't know! Whatever its source, we certainly needed a lot of it to face each day's challenges. Can you imagine the hours we spent learning how to use a tooth brush—a tool so trivial, yet oh-so-useful? Our motto was: *struggle with and against everything!* Struggle—in spite of our caregivers' and teachers' rigidity! Struggle—against medical diagnostics, discouragement and the other kids' cruel and hurtful taunts!

SOCRATES: Tell me, Alexandre, how did you come to philosophy?

ALEXANDRE: I thought that this question, in particular, might interest you. It was precisely in this atmosphere of ubiquitous struggle that I discovered, completely by chance, a work of philosophy that contained the following two phrases: "No one is voluntarily evil" and "Know thyself."

SOCRATES: I've heard this somewhere before …

ALEXANDRE: This existential call immediately resonated with my adolescent self. It turned my life upside down and made it suddenly much more interesting. Everything became a source of reflection. The life-encompassing program it implied felt simultaneously like an exciting adventure, a formidable challenge and an uplifting motivation. From that day on, I set out to gain a better understanding of my peculiar situation and to analyze—in as much detail as possible—our eminent caregivers' and teachers' actions.

SOCRATES: Would you say that what you call 'philosophy' allowed you to view reality in a different light?

ALEXANDRE: Overall, yes—but, most importantly, it allowed me to save my skin, to finally be able to react, to hazard answers, if tentative, to the vexing questions that haunted me. Reading the philosophers nudged me into better understanding, into giving meaning to reality.

SOCRATES: Be more specific. Could you provide an example that illustrates your approach?

ALEXANDRE: Certainly. Let's take an ordinary human faculty such as walking. For many years, I could only crawl on all fours. Little by little, I managed to climb the evolutionary ladder to the point of being able to move around by pushing a kind of wagon that allowed me to keep my balance. But when I was nine and a half, I felt the urge and the need to get rid of this cumber-some crutch. I was given a helmet, and—'marching orders' in hand—off I went!

This is how my great adventure began: stand-ing on my own two feet—"the head as high above the ground as possible," as ethologists put it—I morphed into a true biped … I will never forget the hours I spent shuffling up and down the Center's long, white-washed hallways.

the sincerity of true kindness

ALEXANDRE: One day, as I was precariously staggering about, a friend was closely watching my every move. None of my gestures escaped him. All the while, he was laughing, which really annoyed me. Jean was completely bedridden and much older than I. He could neither talk nor walk, nor even sit up on his own. How did he dare make fun of me—still little—as I was 'stammering' my first independent steps? I just couldn't understand it. Soon, however, I noticed that the more confident my steps became, the more heartily he laughed. And so it was that I passed my entrance exam into the world of bipeds in a hilarious atmosphere of contagious joy. Jean's laughter reached its peak in celebration of my victory.

SOCRATES: Wasn't this a sign?

ALEXANDRE: Walled up in my own pride and prejudice, I didn't know how to read it. But Jean had done everything he could to support me. He knew full well that he would never be able to walk. Motivated by the sincerity of true kindness, he humbly accompanied my each and every step with his sheer presence, without words or gestures. My legs became his legs. It was almost as if he himself was learning to walk.

When, as a teenager, I began attending public school, I encountered very different attitudes. One student's bad grade or mishap would often be the cause of another's joy. It took quite a bit of reflection and observation to make sense of this contrast. Reading philosophy helped me a lot in this. I quickly realized that my environment had changed. I was definitely no longer at the Center, where one person's progress was everybody's.

SOCRATES: How virtuous!

ALEXANDRE: It came naturally.

SOCRATES: Aren't you idealizing a bit here? Your Center sounds like paradise.

ALEXANDRE: Of course, there were conflicts too, but devoid of gratuitous malice.

SOCRATES: Even with the caregivers?

ALEXANDRE: Hm. I have to admit that we weren't very kind to them. Not feeling understood made us aggressive, remorseless even. Which occasionally led to violent altercations. But you have to understand: we were living in a kind of bubble. We didn't have the possibility to step back at will, or talk to a well-meaning, neutral, outside observer. We were literally engaged in a constant power struggle with the staff. The latter, however—being better trained and armed—maintained the upper hand, which made our confrontations especially grueling and partisan. Some of our caregivers excelled at currying favor with the director, who would almost always take their side, making our defeat a foregone conclusion. In this oppressive atmosphere, our families were our last resort. We had to apprise them of the facts and get them to act on our behalf. But how could they have intervened? They never truly understood our predicament. Receiving the bulk of their information from the administration and staff, they mostly had the latter's testimony to go on. When our version of events happened to differ from the official version, we would sometimes be accused of lying.

SOCRATES: Standing up for yourselves, arguing your case—so vital amid all the hardships—didn't this also help you to develop an acute sense of dialogue and reasoned debate?

ALEXANDRE: Yes, but at what cost?

SOCRATES: Wasn't the necessity to engage in dialogue a major asset?

ALEXANDRE: Certainly, but an asset with potentially damaging consequences.

SOCRATES: Sophistry?

ALEXANDRE: More like the ruse and the lie! I am thinking of a particular instance here. I was starving that day; and there, through the staff room's half-opened door, I spy—oh, sweet mirage!—a cake. A magnificent torte, beckoning majestically from the director's desk. The room is strictly off limits. I look right, left, the coast seems clear … I swoop down on my quarry. Woe of woes! The chase ends with the *corpus delicti* splattered all over the rug. Unbearable anxiety takes hold of me. My possible options flit before my mind's eye. How to cover up the crime? Fear of punishment makes me brace for the worst. At first, I attempt to gather it all up with a spoon, then with my bare hands; I try to rub out the stains, but in vain.

Then, a solution presents itself: out the window with this whole mess, both rug and cake. No sooner thought than done! Luckily this happens to be the last day of school before summer break … and nobody could care less!

Living in a community implies respecting a great many rules. With very limited means at our disposal, we had to use cunning tactics to procure even the barest necessities.

SOCRATES: If I understand you correctly, in addition to your motto—*struggle with and against everything!*—you also lived by another precept: *if you want to survive in a hostile environment, be resourceful!*

ALEXANDRE: Yes, but not in a mean, violent or malicious way; more in the spirit of adaptation à la Darwin. We resorted to cunning not in order to do harm or indulge our whims. Far from it, we used it to obtain the most ordinary things—things that every child ought to be able to enjoy as a matter of course. Is it malice to outsmart the teacher to get an extra sip of water?

SOCRATES: In the end, this Darwinian struggle motivated you.

ALEXANDRE: It's true that the obstacles life throws our way can become formative and that a person endowed with even a little bit of common sense will derive greater benefit from them than from all the hefty tomes compiled by education experts. Challenges make you tough, motivate you and force you to come up with solutions. Incidentally, I've been told that children with the same disability will often develop at a different rate depending on their family background. I recall the case of a mother who was severely criticized for trusting her son to ride the train on his own even though he walked more like a robot than an ordinary mortal. I can imagine that it must have been hard for her to let go.

There are mothers who, through excess of love, never allow their children to leave their side. Like contempt, love too can stunt growth. If love becomes a straitjacket, it will stifle the child's abilities. I am not talking about my own, personal experience here, which I wouldn't want to generalize. I simply want to emphasize how important trust has been for me.

SOCRATES: The cake incident reveals the unsuspected resources one might discover at the heart of a difficult situation.

ALEXANDRE: Nietzsche, a member of your guild, often speaks of drawing strength from hardship; he even goes so far as to counsel the benefits of injustice. This approach has greatly helped me. But what a challenge!

embracing our condition

SOCRATES: Going back to what you said earlier, it seems that everything constituted a challenge for you, even the most trivial, everyday
tasks.

ALEXANDRE: Some biologists argue that challenge is the essence of life. At the Center, we
had ample opportunity to ascertain the truth of
this claim. One morning, on my way to trade
school, I was jealously watching the bikers ped-
aling along. I immediately hatched a plan. The
possibilities that this kind of device offered certainly intrigued me.

SOCRATES: But didn't you say that you could
barely stand upright?

ALEXANDRE: That's exactly what the doctor reminded me of, declaring the bicycle "impossible." Unfazed, I told my father about my bold
project … and, after meticulous preparations,
embarked on this hazardous adventure.

Cursing my way through countless hours of
ridiculous practice, I was finally ready for the
big launch. Contrary to medical diagnostics, I
had succeeded in learning to balance on two

wheels. How exhilarating it was from now on to be able to freely roam my local surroundings! On my way to school, heads invariably turned to make sure that this really was the same tottering being they saw every morning.

SOCRATES: Are you saying that you not only had to defy difficulty but the *a prioris*, the preconceptions, we project onto reality as well?

ALEXANDRE: Whence my interest in philosophy. I had to arm myself to combat all the labels that people attached to us. Sartre, another member of your guild, often speaks of "reification" in this context. Reification means being reduced to a thing or attribute, being viewed in terms of a single quality or flaw, being freeze-framed, stunted in one's growth.

SOCRATES: This painful reality, did it feel as palpably oppressive to your companions as well?

ALEXANDRE: As I mentioned before, at the Center friendships formed naturally and without artifice. This allowed us to face the difficulties of our condition together.

SOCRATES: What kinds of difficulty are you referring to?

ALEXANDRE: The Center was teeming with abnormalities: there was I, happily tottering about and slurring my words; there was Philippe, who, at eighteen, stood less than three feet tall; there was Jerôme, who could neither walk nor talk; and Adrien, who was severely intellectually disabled and emitted virtually indecipherable sounds. Nothing united us, and yet everything united us. We were better able to bear the unbearable of our situation as a group, and that's why we made sure not to squander our precious time and resources on useless fussing and bickering. We supported each other the better to rise to the challenge, the better as a group to shoulder the burden of our isolation.

SOCRATES: Could you expand on this idea of mutual support?

ALEXANDRE: Paradoxically, I find it hard to explain. With Adrien, for example, the conversation was limited to "Shirt nice," "Shoe good," "How're ye?"

SOCRATES: Small talk, that's it?

ALEXANDRE: Precisely the opposite. Asking "How are you?" was absolutely vital for us.

SOCRATES: Really?

ALEXANDRE: It's thanks to all the "How-are-you's?" that we were able to take part in each other's lives, shoulder the burden of each other's suffering, communicate our mutual friendship …

SOCRATES: Aren't you exaggerating?

ALEXANDRE: I don't think so. Even though it's obvious that I am describing a very particular situation. But keep in mind that, for the most part, we had difficulty communicating. And so we had to develop our own code, our own language.

Often, at night, thoughts drifting, I would envy the lot of other children. They were sleeping at home, sheltered in the warmth of their families, while I was stuck here, lonely and unprotected. A dim light illuminated our dorm with its curious inhabitants: a dwarf who slept with clenched fists—at twelve he looked like six; a mute who made up for his lack of speech through vigorous snoring; across from me, Jerôme, watching me attentively with piercing eyes. One time, exerting a superhuman effort, he asked me, in his barely audible voice: "How're ye?"

To this day, I am overwhelmed by the very thought that Jerôme, paralyzed and confined to his bed, would take an interest in my petty worries. He didn't preach courage or the necessity to think positively in the vein of so much self-help literature; yet, his simple question— "How're ye?"—said it all. His support was unconditional.

We tend to exclude the different, the useless, the stranger, the other … Jerôme wasn't capable of doing anything physically. Given his limitations, he was often referred to as "unprofitable." Yet it was he, more than anyone else, who taught me the difficult craft of being human.

SOCRATES: What exactly do you mean by this expression?

ALEXANDRE: At the Center, we quickly learned that when it comes to living, you can never rest on your laurels. Every single day we had to get back to work, solve problems, one by one, embrace our condition, pick ourselves up and keep going. This was our daily labor, our true vocation—what I call, for lack of a better term, the craft of being human.

drawing strength from our weakness

ALEXANDRE: The human condition has always astonished, fascinated me. But at the Center reality was sometimes hard to accept. Our daily life offered plenty of occasions for despairing of our condition.

SOCRATES: Is it because humanity's weakness and misery stand out more than its greatness and strength?

ALEXANDRE: At the Center, there was neither poetry nor literature that would have taught us to appreciate human greatness. Our daily spectacle presented misery above all: illness, loneliness, suffering, death.

SOCRATES: Does this really prevent us from apprehending the beauty of the human condition?

ALEXANDRE: No. My peers—Jerôme and many others—raised me. And in their own way, they all contributed to revealing human greatness to me; not through individual acts, but through their very being. What many an eminent psychologist tried to inculcate in me in long and exceedingly learned discourses, Jerôme imparted in the most simple manner, through his sheer presence. He inspired me to explore my own history, my weaknesses, my own humanity.

When he asked me how I was doing, Jerôme simply wanted to let me know that he was happy that I existed, that he existed—despite our rotten lot. Jerôme plumbed the depths of reality in order to assume it wholly and completely. He showed me that in order to accept our condition, we have to draw strength and sustenance from our own lived experience, from our very weakness … No pedagogue or caregiver has ever been able to teach me that.

SOCRATES: What did they propose?

ALEXANDRE: They told me to choose role models and follow their lead, never to search too deep within myself for illuminating answers, least of all at the most visceral level of my fears and anxieties.

But let's get back to the others. Adrien, too, has given me a lot; he was the universal object of ridicule, the 'village simpleton', the one you could taunt unpunished. His boundless generosity, his infinite kindness made him vulnerable and exposed him to abuse. Many took advantage of him.

SOCRATES: You too?

ALEXANDRE: Unfortunately, yes!

SOCRATES: But tell me more about the ways in which you were able to lean on him?

ALEXANDRE: Full of joy, content and eager to help, Adrien not only assisted me with my daily chores, but he was also an infinite source of encouragement. His presence, meanwhile, was as discreet and self-effacing as can be. His conversation, as you already know, didn't exceed simple exchanges such as "Oh," "In bed," and "Shirt nice." In spite of this, however, or rather because of it, he greatly surpassed me. I sought and found support, openness and strength in him. His very presence was much more important than his actions. I think of him every time someone tells me that what really matters are one's career and social status.

When I think about what our actions truly mean, a friendship like Adrien's stands out as a true beacon. With increasing urgency, the question arises: where do the elderly, the orphan, the AIDS victim, the prostitute fit in? At the Center, all of us, no matter how destitute, fit in.

SOCRATES: That's interesting: you were living in an extremely complex environment, surrounded by a group of unique characters. Yet, according to what you are saying, everything appears to have been relatively simple.

ALEXANDRE: Existing was already difficult

enough, why further complicate it? That would have been a luxury. Simple words afforded us affection. And that was enough. Our mutual presence and gestures of kindness meant more than anything, in a very essential way.

SOCRATES: Is that why the body was so important?

ALEXANDRE: The body was our preferred means of communion. We made contact with our eyes or through simple gestures rather than endless conversation. We all came from such different places! Everyone brought his own, unique experiences with him—experiences that are difficult to describe, as you can imagine. Moreover, we didn't always have the means necessary to express them in words. Yes, our existence was unusual, frightening and beautiful at the same time. A look, a gesture could suffice to mitigate our isolation, to build a bridge between our separate worlds. When I left the Center, I carried the warmth that drew us together inside me. It took me a long time and a lot of energy to learn that in this 'other world' gestures play a very different role and can mean very different things. At first, I didn't understand this.

ALEXANDRE: The sense of shame drilled into us at the Center led to an excessive, and not at all healthy, separation of the sexes, and …

SOCRATES: Interesting! That's where simplicity was no longer appropriate. You lived mostly among boys.

ALEXANDRE: Which had grave consequences. My lack of contact with girls obviously constituted a critical deficit.

SOCRATES: Could you be more specific?

ALEXANDRE: In trade school, the first time I talked to the girl who everybody thought was the most beautiful, I was literally mesmerized by her grace—not by her beauty, which others talked about and were superficially drawn to, so much as by a certain inner force and gentle nobility. So bewitched was I that I jumped at her and squeezed her so tightly that we collapsed on top of each other. In stark contrast to what I had felt, the bystanders' looks betrayed something ambiguous, alarming and impure. This entire incident saddened and humiliated me: I realized that in this new world one's loneliness was even more difficult to communicate than at the Center.

A friend whispered in my ear: "You blew this one big time, maybe it's worth seriously re-thinking your strategy." This really hurt, and it still hurts when I think back to this misadventure. I am still not totally convinced that gestures need to be suppressed. It seems to me that many of the social norms that call for restraint derive above all from fear of and uneasiness with the body and the other person. Even today, I sometimes have to restrain the occasional, ostensibly overfamiliar gesture in my interaction with professors, for instance. Given my druthers, I'd sometimes instinctively and spontaneously express my affection and admiration by shaking their hand or patting them on the back. But I know full well that such gestures will be considered inappropriate or even taboo in certain situations.

SOCRATES: And your new strategy?

ALEXANDRE: All of these events made me realize that I belonged to a 'different world'. Which is why it was paramount to join in and integrate, learn the language, codes and prohibitions of *this* world. I began by observing.

SOCRATES: Observing is probably the philosopher's foremost skill, and more generally …

ALEXANDRE: For sure. And so I started closely examining those creatures that were so different from me, in an attempt to be accepted by people who were one head taller and ran ten times faster than I. Listening to them, you got the impression that they were the smoothest-operating Casanovas, ever out-speeding the cops on their scooters. And then there was I: tottering, helpless, and on foot. I quickly realized that the more upbeat, dynamic and funny I was, the easier it would be for me to fit in.

I got busy learning how to wield words, make them laugh. And soon enough, to everybody's great surprise, I had earned my place among them. Interestingly, my real friends weren't among the top of the class, nor were they among the conformist, obedient ones—far from it: they were among the slackers, the pranksters and troublemakers in the last row, who could be quite cruel at times. But even they treated me with a kindness, innocence and affection that I haven't ever been able to find elsewhere. Their way of helping and interacting with me had something pristine and unadulterated about it. It wasn't the pity of old ladies who'd sometimes give me change (which, by the way, I didn't mind at all), nor was it like the son's ostentatious solicitude for a parent, eagerly displaying his good upbringing and *savoir-vivre*. Theirs was a clumsy, discreet, and sincere friendship. They confided in me, and I opened up to them.

I still remember one of those rebels whom I used to greet with the words: "Be good!" One day, he bluntly replied: "And you, walk straight!" This pleased me to no end. He respected me for who I was and didn't treat me with kid gloves like those who inanely smile at me from behind the till when I pay for my instant meal of spaghetti with herbs.

SOCRATES: All of this would seem to suggest that pity hurts more than contempt?

ALEXANDRE: Exactly! No more pity. Here again, I agree with Nietzsche. I think he was spot on when he condemned the hypocrisy of pity. Virtually every day I come across those well-meaning, condescending looks that are supposed to make me feel better but actually deny my liberty and, consequently, me as a person.

SOCRATES: Hm. How exactly is it that you feel your liberty is being denied by pity?

ALEXANDRE: I think that contempt motivates, as Balzac once said … Pity, by contrast, due to its blandness, anesthetizes. One day, I was out and about with a friend who could only move around on a power scooter. Happy to have escaped our caregivers' ever-reproachful eye, we were freely roaming the city streets on his scooter. Here and there, people began poking out the windows, curious about this unusual, motorized pair.

We felt liberated and belted out our happiness at the top of our lungs. Once again, our institutional past caught up with us, costing us dearly: at the Center, whenever we felt joy or happiness, we absolutely needed to share it; and in order to do so, we had to express our emotions in a very demonstrative fashion.

As we were zigzagging across the lawns along the road, our heads turned skyward, a group of toothless retirees began following our every move through their bifocals. Soon enough they had surrounded us and were closely observing us from all sides. So what! Our outing was all that mattered! Until, suddenly, a police car put an end to our ear-splitting parcours. An officer emerged from the vehicle and requested that we immediately return to the Center. Our liberty had been nipped in the bud! We were forced to go back. The retirees' pity and misplaced concern had done more harm than good. SOCRATES: Good conscience alone is not enough.

ALEXANDRE: That's exactly what Nietzsche says.

(*Socrates remains silent*)

That night, I asked myself the fundamental question if I might be less free than others—if there would always be people who, despite their inhibitions, would remind me, in complete good faith, that I was disabled.

SOCRATES: Good conscience, then, is really not enough, and everyone can see it. After all, the three hundred and sixty-one judges who sentenced me to death only did what they had to in their official function—in good conscience.

ALEXANDRE: As elsewhere, at the Center, too, authority—or rather the mask of authority—was tied to function. The *doctor* was respected without his competence being questioned. The *teacher* knew 'everything'. The *caregiver*—presumably endowed with omniscience—felt obliged to instruct my parents in the art of child rearing.

For a long time, the Center's motto was: "The parents have brought a disabled child into this world. If they give it to us, we will turn it into a more or less normal person." And when confronted with the mask of another's authority, the employees didn't hesitate to dissimulate their smallness of heart. This made many parents insecure and lose trust. Endeavoring to reassure the parents, the caregivers excelled at the art of flattery. I still recall all the attention I'd receive on the days immediately preceding annual parents' visiting day. We may have been too young, and our mental faculties not always up to par, but it didn't take us long to see through this charade. We used it to recharge our batteries, without ignoring the ephemeral and illusory nature of such respite.

Not surprisingly, our relations with the staff remained superficial. We never got to the point of engaging with them from one person to another; the most we could hope for was the professional's interaction with the child, the doctor's with the patient.

SOCRATES: What about people outside the Center?

ALEXANDRE: They tended to project negative images onto us. Often, when I'd pass them on the street, townsfolk would begin whispering, elbowing each other: "Poor boy! Poor little one!" They almost succeeded in making me lose my bearings. But deep down, I was convinced that I was actually quite fortunate: I had wonderful parents, true friends, and good playmates … Still, being thus put into doubt, the certainty that I wasn't actually more unhappy than others was in danger of corroding.

I was subconsciously aware that for many people my very presence represented a kind of failure or accident. For them, I embodied the kind of suffering that made them feel guilty, almost responsible for my disability. I played the part of their guilty conscience.

On a number of occasions, I noticed how passers-by would fall silent at the sight of me, assuming an air of sympathy, a bit like doffing one's hat at the sight of a hearse. Then, as soon as I had walked by, the conversation would resume. Was it simply a reflex? I don't know.

SOCRATES: And you never had this kind of reaction?

ALEXANDRE: Actually, I did catch myself once feeling something similar at the sight of a blind person. I had projected onto another all the anxiety, fear and unease that difference can engender. Inexperienced as I was, I couldn't have explained this type of complex emotional response, whose ultimate source, I'm sure, must be sought deep within oneself. My friends and I were steeped in this kind of atmosphere. On our 'day off', during our weekly Wednesday afternoon outings, our caregivers didn't exactly improve things either. What the passers-by witnessed was a procession of gimps, wheelchair-bound cripples, dwarfs, paralytics and other kooks. They'd watch us helplessly, experiencing, I'm sure, the most conflicting, inexpressible emotions.

SOCRATES: Which is quite understandable?

ALEXANDRE: Nowadays, it's all about integration. In those days, it was all about immersion: one group thrown in with another, and both remaining comfortably and conveniently separated, without dialogue or communication. A snail slithering through the grass under the inquisitive, slightly disgusted gaze of the child playing in the park: my companions and I were this snail. As for the child, it represents the entire social sphere: the men and women who go shopping, to the doctor's, pay bills, run into each other on the street.

Unconsciously, I carried this image of the snail around with me for a long time, ending up identifying with it. If 'Wednesday' once evoked joy and excitement, today it belongs to my less than joyful memories …

SOCRATES: Are you frustrated?

ALEXANDRE: When, as a child, you're trying to grow and flourish in an environment that constantly treats you as unworthy (often involuntarily), you wind up internalizing this kind of projection and all the things you've heard.

Many of us were in danger of losing our spontaneous trust in life. Incidentally, according to recent research, the first words a newborn hears have an unsuspected impact on its development.

Hegel repeatedly stresses the significance of the other's gaze. Encountering the other, he argues, enables us to elevate ourselves, grow and become fully human … Throughout his works, and especially in the play *No Exit*, Sartre, too, highlights our visceral, profound need to be seen and acknowledged by the other, a need that is never satisfied.

(*Socrates remains silent*)

The other's gaze, I am convinced, constructs and structures our personality. But it can also damage, condemn, hurt.

SOCRATES: I imagine that you have many a story to share?

ALEXANDRE: I'm taking a walk with a friend. In a hushed voice, she tells me that she wanted to commit suicide.

We walk past a boy of about sixteen. He gives my friend a disdainful look, scans me from head to toe, then says to her: "Did you forget the leash?" Taken aback, my friend experiences a violent sense of revolt.

SOCRATES: What about you?

ALEXANDRE: Me? I attempt to calm her, telling her that she ought to forgive him, that he acted out of ignorance, out of a desire to …

SOCRATES: How do you personally deal with this kind of mockery?

ALEXANDRE: I, for one, believe that it is rooted in misdirected, mismanaged weakness. Being aware of this helps me. Often, a group will evince greater cruelty than a person alone, who might do no more than laugh at you. A cocky teenager flanked by his acolytes, on the other hand, laughs with pointed aggression. Perhaps, in so doing he hopes to demonstrate his self-confidence and superiority; not to mention his fear of the 'snail', which he must cover up. This way, he can also avoid commiserating or feeling pity. Everybody deals with discomfort in his own way. The residual damages of mockery, the need to belong, the necessity to find meaning even in painful experiences have taught me to observe the behavior of others—and certainly my own—very closely.

SOCRATES: How have the philosophers helped you?

ALEXANDRE: The philosophers have been of great help—not through their answers so much as through their very method, their field of inquiry. I find it hard to explain their precious support any other way! For me, philosophy is a kind of magnifying glass for observing reality, for making sense of the day-to-day, for finding meaning in experience. Very early on, I felt the need to understand the cruelty that sometimes marks human relations, the precariousness of man's condition.

SOCRATES: Tell me, Alexandre, are you referring to 'human being' in general, or do you mean 'man' as opposed to 'woman'—a topic you don't seem to be inclined to broach? Is this yet another point of frustration?

ALEXANDRE: How can one talk about something one doesn't know? I am hardly an expert in this domain.

the joy of being alive

SOCRATES: You have barely spoken about school.

ALEXANDRE: I could tell you all about my first day in trade school. I skulked along the hallways trying to remain as inconspicuous as possible, to disappear in the crowd. What a fool's errand! Me, trying to remain inconspicuous! I got it right away: I had to fight for my place at the school.

Pressed against the radiator during my very first period, which happened to be French, I bitterly regretted not being able to hide in the closet. I was closely watching each of the alien creatures that would from now on constitute my world. Then the teacher asked the following question: "Do the same causes always have the same effects?" Silence. After several moments' hesitation, with a lump in my throat, I raised my hand and said: "No! If you trip going down the stairs, you can break one or both legs, even though the cause will be the same each time …" "That's a good example," the teacher said. And in defiance of all the looks intently directed at me, I added: "It's a matter of experience, monsieur." At which point the entire class burst into laughter.

Integration completed! Three pleasant years followed … At recess, I was greeted with smiles and received a couple of friendly pats on the back. The pranksters realized that the stranger was one of them. The smart and ambitious ones respected me for being the first to respond. Everything had been gained. How little it takes sometimes! Proving myself was vital.

One of my classmates had a misshapen thumb. He always kept his hand in his pocket. I told him: "Don't try to hide your disability. Look at me, I would have to walk around wrapped in a garbage bag!" Very quickly I realized that attempting to hide one's disability leads to isolation. It's there, and one must accept it like an extra limb, come to terms with it. To achieve this, knowing one's weaknesses is key …

SOCRATES: Isn't your praise of weakness somewhat self-serving and complacent?

ALEXANDRE: It is vital! Coming to terms with it is the only way to go since, anyway, "we are irrevocably in this boat," as Pascal would say.

Too many people focus exclusively on the grim, negative aspects of our situation, without seeing its potential. They only see the snail in the disabled person, or, more generally, in the person who is different.

I cannot explain this strange phenomenon. The events I am relating have caused acute suffering. Ubiquitous loneliness, being separated from our families, indescribable pain: this was our daily lot. On Sundays, I'd start crying three hours before having to part from my parents and brother again. Riding the bus back to the Center, I'd look out the window and count each meter that was taking me further away from my mother. Despite all that, or maybe because of it, however, we were also often joyful and happy about the small things. This contentment dominated our entire existence and took on different forms: from the sheer joy of being alive, to the joy of having companions to face hardships with, to the joy of having parents who loved us. Why obliterate these 'good spirits'—especially now that I had finally joined the ranks of the 'normal'?

At the Center, the simple things in daily life— a smile, a good dessert—brought on the feeling of happiness. Life's sweetness in its pristine simplicity reminded us that we ought to enjoy it, all obstacles and hardships notwithstanding. Life wasn't a rival; it was an ally. An exacting, severe ally, to be sure, but an ally still. Of course, we weren't consciously aware of it, we simply lived it day by day.

Adrien is a prime example of this attitude. Intellectually disabled, he didn't know how to read or write and could only mumble a couple of words. In his language, which I picked up in time, 'mamaya' for instance meant 'I am going to my mom'. He had invented his own code for each thing. Surprisingly, he was easy to understand once you got used to it.

SOCRATES: Like a foreign language?

ALEXANDRE: Obviously, the things he wanted to say remained fairly simple. His attention to others, however, was astonishing. Not a single detail of his environment escaped him. He observed those around him with admiration. He was happy contemplating the beautiful things others had. It was his way of showing attachment and affection. His intellectual abilities were not sufficiently developed to allow him to properly verbalize his feelings. In saying "Shirt nice" or "Good hair," he succeeded in expressing, in his own simple terms, his kindness and friendship, his joy about being together. And yes, this *was* vital.

Adrien's concern for Jerôme, in particular, moved me deeply. He cared for Jerôme with such unremitting solicitude that it almost

seemed as though a different Adrien were helping Jerôme. No longer the maladroit, oafish
Adrien, but a subtle Adrien who knew just what
to do to put Jerôme back in his bed. Above all,
he mustn't fall! This scene still impresses me.
Adrien's instinctual delicacy resembled that of a
tigress curbing her own aggression to suckle
her cubs.

He always viewed the other as different, as a
source of astonishment and wonder. His interlocutors always became subjects of genuine
communication, communion even. Here again,
weakness, the inability to speak, was in search
of a path to surpass itself. Adrien established
dialogue not through the intermediary of language but through his very being, a source of
joy.

Unfortunately, his desire to do good made
him very vulnerable as well, and others took advantage of him. The children in his village in-
cited him to do stupid things. For instance,
they'd tell him to smash windows or drop his
pants in the middle of the street, and Adrien
would do it, merely wishing to belong.

He did sense that the things they wanted him
to do were somehow out of the ordinary and
only complied in the hope of becoming part of
the group. His overflowing love tolerated even

humiliation. Exuberant, joyful, endowed with an unrivaled personality, Adrien couldn't contain his love's over-abundance.

But his unusual emotional responses were also perceived as shocking. The neighbors had barbed-wire fences put up around their properties in order to get rid of the intruder.

SOCRATES: Yet again: fear of difference.

ALEXANDRE: Difference may be troubling and disconcerting in our desire for perfection. Fear, on the other hand, is constricting. Adrien wasn't only disparaged by his 'playmates', who made fun of him, but also, and above all, by those do-gooders who will donate a hundred Francs a month to Madagascar. All Adrien wanted was to share his love and friendship, nothing else mattered.

Adrien didn't have a good memory: for instance, he couldn't remember his telephone number; but he'd as easily forget anybody's wrongdoing. Always seeing the good in others, he knew the price of friendship.

SOCRATES: When you say 'knew', you mean a kind of intuitive, lived knowledge?

ALEXANDRE: Yes, for Adrien this knowledge was worth more than any philosophy. It was vivifying, a source of joy …

SOCRATES: But isn't Adrien an exception?

ALEXANDRE: Not really. I remember this one radiant girl at the public pool. She was peacefully doing backstrokes. What a contrast to her actual story—the most gruesome I've ever heard. She had lived in Africa, in a war-torn country. Soldiers had ransacked her village and hacked up her mother and father with axes. They had left her amid a mound of mutilated, blood-soaked bodies, arms and legs strewn about pell-mell. Can there be a more horrific situation? And yet, watching her float on her back—with that eternal smile on her face—she seemed to embody the most complete joy, absolute bliss. Amazing how capable of adapting we are!

SOCRATES: Darwin again?

ALEXANDRE: Much better! Life's challenges are more formative by far than the clean-cut proofs of eminent scientists and pedagogues caught up in their abstractions.

SOCRATES: Aren't you justifying suffering?

ALEXANDRE: I am simply saying that one has to do everything in one's power to find some benefit even in the most dire and destructive circumstances. I insist on the usefulness of challenges, if only because they are unavoidable. There is no point in engaging in endless conversation about suffering. It either needs to

be eliminated or, if that's impossible, accepted
and endowed with meaning.

they talked and analyzed

ALEXANDRE: Our caregivers assembled frequently: there were constant meetings, minutes, inspections, seminars! I was always struck by the number of hours they spent in the staff room drinking coffee and eating cookies. They talked and talked …

SOCRATES: But isn't this a good way to address problems?

ALEXANDRE: Maybe, but one that wasn't often productively employed. For hours on end, they'd analyze, comment, and expatiate on our most insignificant actions and gestures. How much time they devoted to it! But woe to the one among us who dared to hold them up as they were getting ready to leave for the day because he needed to go to the bathroom! It meant running the risk of being reduced to yet another clinical case likely to become the bracing subject of brilliant analysis.

There are two thick folders at the Center—I'll return to them later—in which generations of caregivers, doctors, and acne-faced interns have compiled an inventory of my existence and recorded their views on my situation, my parents …

SOCRATES: And what do these ominous folders say?

ALEXANDRE: I don't know. In a way, I'm glad I don't! For although, by inscrutable decree, the folders were theoretically open to the entire care-giving staff—from the inexperienced intern to the seasoned doctor—the principal concerned, the actual subject of those records, was barred from accessing them! Just think of it: a throng of professionals erecting an impressive theoretical edifice. Perhaps they felt the need to discuss and speculate in order to fill a void, make up for their lack of experience, or cover up their inadequacy.

How much energy wasted on trying to explain trifles! A simple headache spawned speculations worthy of a Lacan. Everyone strove to come up with his version of the facts. I remember one friend who was wearing braces that cut into his gums. He told me that his dad had to use pliers to remove them. The Center's dentist, who hadn't taken his complaints seriously, had chalked the pain up to a psychological cause, preferring a ludicrous explanation to admitting a professional slip-up.

I knew disabled people who developed serious illnesses due, in no small part, to the fact that their doctors didn't carry their examinations far enough, contenting themselves rather with pseudo-psychological explanations. Here again, a concrete instance that warrants taking a hard look at the human condition.

Pascal emphasizes that we are both body and mind, and cannot be reduced to either. Both interact with each other. "Man is neither angel nor beast. Our misfortune is that he who wishes to act the angel acts the beast." Far from elevating us, denying the body degrades us. Denying the mind: same thing!

Achieving harmony between these two dimensions and knowing how to harness it, therein precisely lies the difficult apprenticeship of the craft of being human. It behooves us to constantly strive to surpass ourselves, to persist in endeavoring to go beyond what we already are, to ceaselessly engender ourselves and further perfect what has already self-realized within us. This insight assumed radical importance for me early on. Happiness—if it exists— is thus diametrically opposed to any kind of quiet, tranquil, and tepid comfort. It demands intense activity, perpetual struggle; it resembles the disinterested, selfless plenitude acquired in permanent combat …

SOCRATES: That is precisely the philosopher's task …

ALEXANDRE: There have certainly been many attempts to define wisdom, and we have to be careful and, above all, not give in to cliché. Personally, I know very little about it. For me, being wise means knowing and accepting one's possibilities and weaknesses, facing and assuming one's reality head-on. It takes a long apprenticeship to get there. As the Stoics used to say, wisdom requires a constancy of commitment that is only rarely achieved. This kind of committed acceptance demands rigorous work on oneself, which, in my view, by far exceeds psychoanalytic introspection.

A fair number of people who have undergone analysis come out finding themselves in a state of utter malaise and perplexity after being 'cured'.

SOCRATES: Let's not digress. What did your caregivers aim to accomplish?

ALEXANDRE: Nothing specific, really. They sought to alleviate rather than heal. They treated the symptoms without endeavoring to understand the underlying causes in order to eradicate them once and for all. I had a similar experience with several doctors. For a long time, I suffered from migraines. The doctors' opinions on my condition were painfully at odds with each other: according to one, it was a symptom of anxiety, while another insisted on chronic pathology … Then, one day, a friend of mine who happened to be a physical therapist massaged my neck, which greatly helped me. He quickly diagnosed muscular hypertension due to excessive reading. Once the root cause had been identified, it was easy to cure. This trivial example shows that *a prioris* can have unhappy consequences. Doctors, caregivers commit many an error due to incompetence, indolence, ignorance, and other subtle forms of *a priori*.

But to get back to the folders I spoke of earlier: they were chock-full of all kinds of stylistic exercise. One of the more congenial staff members let me read a couple of lines. What I found were judgments about my parents, pseudo-psychoanalytical explanations of my behavior, medical reports going out of their way to declare the use of a typewriter "counter-indicated" in my case, even though I can barely write my own name legibly by hand.

SOCRATES: And nobody did anything?

ALEXANDRE: At their meetings, the caregivers

were more concerned with convincing themselves of their own altruism and integrity ...

I have since become very suspicious of meetings in which everyone advances his own view-
point ... But don't think that I feel deep-seated
resentment toward my caregivers. I owe them a
lot too. Thanks to some of them I learned to
walk, button my pants ... Still, their overall incompetence and complacency caused a lot of
damage.

SOCRATES: Tell me more about the ones who
helped you, the ones you appreciated! This will
allow me to form a more complete, objective
opinion.

ALEXANDRE: Those were the ones who loved
and believed in us, who saw our potential. They
didn't pretend to have everything under control, were aware that many aspects of our
predicament escaped them, and showed mod-
esty. More pragmatically minded than some of
their colleagues, they didn't reduce reality to
idle abstractions and futile theories. They acted
as philosophers, following reality's lead, attempting to understand us as best they could.

SOCRATES: Be more concrete.

ALEXANDRE: Matthieu, for instance, who had
been a carpenter before switching to special education, handled problems with ease. A practi-

cal, hands-on person, he tackled each difficulty one by one. When he was around, meetings were short, efficient and productive. His method resembled yours. He believed in education from the ground up, starting with the individual. He had confidence in us and encouraged us to recognize and acknowledge our illusions, penchants, and weaknesses.

Like you, he held that the solutions we are looking for are already within us and that they merely need to be brought to light. Matthieu didn't propound an abstract theory divorced from reality; he awakened us to the knowledge we already carried inside, to our own dormant abilities.

SOCRATES: That's a good definition of the teacher.

ALEXANDRE: Yes, I guess ... The good teacher is a midwife, one who asks questions and uncovers abilities buried underneath various obstacles. This, in turn, requires absolute faith in the other, and also humility—the requisite humility that allows one to keep a certain distance, not to judge the other, to be aware that the other will always and irreducibly remain a singular human being who can never be fully imposed on, analyzed, or understood.

SOCRATES: How has this benefited you?

ALEXANDRE: Matthieu only stayed on for one year, but our progress during that time surpassed all our preceding labors. Under his guidance, I finally became aware of my own responsibility. From that moment on—and with external support, to be sure—I was finally able to embark upon my own proper education.

Matthieu taught us that life itself—and by 'life' I mean concrete experience—hands us the problem-solving tools we need, which gradually come into view in the course of an ongoing dialogue: with friends, relatives, and, above all, ourselves.

SOCRATES: How exactly was this so important?

ALEXANDRE: Many employees at the Center insisted on maintaining a strict distance between 'patient' and caregiver. This 'harmless' practice led to much gratuitous suffering.

SOCRATES: Why are you complaining? Haven't you spoken in favor of suffering just now?

ALEXANDRE: I am not complaining. It's just that it was enough if an intern my age should become friendly with me for a higher-up to advise against it and call it off immediately, which made relations very perfunctory, 'clinical' almost. All in all, this mandated distance presented a radical obstacle to our education.

SOCRATES: Wasn't this demonstrative will to

distance based on unacknowledged fear?

ALEXANDRE: No doubt. All the same, this distance moved us further away from our caregivers. How do you confide in and share personal matters with people who insist on remaining aloof? Which is why we never got to address any real problems with them. As far as I'm concerned, they were technocrats, specialists; what I needed, however, was a friendly ear, a warm presence that would have fostered problem-solving as a team.

This distance ended up creating an unbridgeable gulf between us and them. It's true that a certain detachment can help the caregiver to safeguard his or her privacy, to not get overwhelmed by the patient's predicament. But there is a big difference between the reasonable and necessary distance born of experience and a distance willfully and insensitively imposed. All this is a matter …

SOCRATES: … of precarious balance.

ALEXANDRE: Social work often attracts people who look for validation. The caregiver's profession, in particular, gives its practitioners the opportunity to take on a role that allows them to prove themselves. They wear their work on their sleeve, so to speak, and virtually enjoy special status.

I have often encountered deft debaters among them with rigid, unpredictable personalities; they had no sense of humor, tolerated nothing, got annoyed easily, and dispensed advice they didn't follow themselves. Still, they worked hard to pass as authorities. One spent all of his time and energy buttering up the director. Another crisscrossed the entire city in a wheelchair in order to gain a 'phenomenological' understanding of what it means to be disabled. I won't even bother telling you about the woman who went into social work because her chronic allergies prevented her from pursuing her true dream: dressage. I also recall one caregiver who, when he was told that his "job must be really tough," merely held his hand demonstratively to his heart.

SOCRATES: It doesn't seem to me that you are really over it. You are laughing about it now, but ...

ALEXANDRE: I felt humiliated, ill at ease. Were we nothing but a chore, a burden, a 'job' to be done? On the street, however, if they happened to run into someone they knew, our caregivers would grab our hands, as if demonstratively to emphasize their superhuman efforts in attempting to 'civilize' and entertain us.

Jean-Marc, for example, took me to the disco with him a couple of times. He introduced me to all his female friends and explained what kind of work he was 'performing on me'. I felt like a rare, exotic specimen, exhibited to titillate and impress the audience. Wasn't he the epitome of fecklessness? How could I have been angry with him? Thanks to me, Jean-Marc achieved his goal of becoming the object of undeserved veneration. Whenever he ran into me on the street, he made sure to pat me on the back for all his friends to see, and to declare, "I know him," before proceeding to extol the nobility of his profession.

How different from Sebastian, whom I first met when he was an intern at the Center. One day, we ran into each other on the street, and I told my friends from trade school: "He used to be one of my teachers at the Center." "What a peculiar choice of introduction," he later told me. "The Center was certainly the place where we met, but our relationship can't be reduced to that; I consider you a good acquaintance." For him, our relationship wasn't just that between caregiver and disabled. He didn't act like a professional with me but like a friend.

SOCRATES: In his own way, then, he had solved the problem of distance.

83

ALEXANDRE: Yes, and brilliantly at that. The special education teacher's job requires deep personal involvement; at the same time, it mustn't completely absorb him. He has to foster his student's autonomy. It's not a job like other jobs in that mistakes can have fatal, irreversible consequences.

SOCRATES: Can you give me concrete examples? What might be obvious to you isn't necessarily obvious to me. I imagine it must have been difficult for you …

ALEXANDRE: Sure! I can list a number of mistakes that have been particularly aggravating. Let's begin with our finances. At the Center, whatever money we had, we had to put in a communal cash box. It's certainly an honorable idea, but it can also lead to excesses that I'm still paying for today.

Every week, I received a modest allowance that I could spend at will. At the end of the week, I was supposed to return whatever was left to the caregiver in charge, who would then put it back in the box. But to the child that I was then, returning the money was equal to forfeiting it, which is why my fiscal policy could be boiled down to the motto: "Spend all you've got!"

Thus, I would often ask that the candy be cut in half at the confectioner's if I still had any change left in my purse—a habit I had a hard time breaking. Sure, I can put a positive spin on it by saying that to me money was merely a means rather than an end in itself. The flip side of the coin, though, was a bit more difficult to sustain …

Another, much more serious, mistake: many of us lacked self-confidence. Our social workers, however—even though they came equipped with a highly sophisticated and varied psychological toolkit acquired in years of study—tended to gloss over the problem …

SOCRATES: Could it be that all their 'expertise' actually affected your self-confidence in a negative way?

ALEXANDRE: More often than not, they didn't know how to put their theories to practical use, how to adapt them to the demands of concrete situations.

I'll never forget one caregiver who, after consulting a work of popular psychology, decided to round us up in one room. We were so excited about it and couldn't wait to find out what she was planning to do! Our rabbit ears pricked up, we were expecting to witness the event of the century. Our disappointment was the graver for it! This eminent Freudian, well versed in all the secrets of the human soul, solemnly invited us to "hold a wake for our lives."

She must have consulted a work that touted the necessity to withdraw from the problems of existence. However, in not taking into account our particular situation, she had completely misunderstood the lessons the work had to offer.

I am sure that she merely wished to direct our attention to the fragility of our bodies, to the precariousness of our futures. But she did it so clumsily! For we were already very much aware of our weakness, our singular predicament, the uncertainty of what life had in store for us. "You will never be Maradona," she chose to tell me specifically. I only thought, "Screw Maradona, I never wanted to be like him in the first place!" These and similar obstacles notwithstanding, we fervently continued to fight for every bit of progress we could possibly make, difficult though it may be.

What needs to be remembered is that children and teenagers have much greater strength and resilience than one tends to give them credit for. This caregiver, motivated by good intentions, only wished to protect us from falling prey to idealizing, fantasy, and envy. But nature has its own way of arranging things and is second to none in dispensing its own counsel.

SOCRATES: How did you find this out?

ALEXANDRE: We knew instinctively that having our heads in the clouds was dangerous. Whenever we indulged in fantasizing, the shock of the real would rudely call us back to order. At the same time, we also understood the perils of doing nothing, of only seeing the difficulty without looking to the solution, without believing in eventual success.

SOCRATES: This particular caregiver's mistake certainly had a good influence on you, then?

ALEXANDRE: Indeed, despite everything, there was an upside to her lesson. I've often said that I have been educated *a contrario* in being presented with rigid, cookie-cutter behavioral models that I've tried my best *not* to follow.

(They both laugh)

All in all, however, our caregivers' influence did bear fruit. But you had to have a certain freedom of spirit to reap its benefits. If our challenges had been insurmountable, if we had had to wage a never-ending war in a completely hostile environment, or hadn't had the rare possibility to step back, bear witness and reflect on what was happening to us at the Center, this kind of critique would have been impossible.

culture shock

SOCRATES: Alexandre, could you dig a little deeper into how your years at the Center have affected you?

ALEXANDRE: Life outside the Center was formative for me. It revealed my reflexes. I became aware that part of what I had been taught ran counter to my flourishing, to living in society at large. But not all of us had this opportunity to begin with. Those of us who only sporadically ventured outside faced a twofold challenge: getting integrated into an alien environment, and, concomitantly, having to unlearn certain behaviors that stood in the way of integration.

I wouldn't want to denigrate my life at the Center, for it gave me so much! My erstwhile companions will forever remain unforgettable friends.

SOCRATES: What kinds of difficulty have you encountered since you left?

ALEXANDRE: Our lives had been strictly regulated. My departure from the Center was marked by a veritable culture shock. I had to learn all the routines, customs, and rules of my new life from scratch.

When someone asked me if I liked this or that band, I didn't even know that it was a band. I didn't know the most common colloquialisms. I remember one time when a friend told me that he "smoked weed"; I only thought that I must have landed on the wrong planet. But I quickly realized that I had to become fluent in *their* language and bone up on *their* habits if I wanted to integrate successfully.

Nowadays, more and more children with disabilities get integrated into the regular curriculum early on so as to avoid these types of predicament. A number of parents have told me that early integration carries a dual benefit: it allows the disabled child to develop more seamlessly, while at the same time enjoining its classmates to quickly shed their initial, more or less overt, attitude of rejection. And before you know it, initial mockery and derision give way to lasting friendships.

Here's one particular memory: a father told me once that his daughter had messed up her leg braces and was afraid of going back to school. She simply couldn't face her classmates' stares. The father, however, insisted, with a heavy heart, that she return to school, and the daughter had to oblige. After their initial surprise, the other kids accepted her in the most natural way. Children have this amazing ability to overcome both initial fear and mockery. They are much more capable of integrating, coming to terms with and accepting difference than adults.

SOCRATES: Are you sure?

ALEXANDRE: I believe so. But I also think that education has an essential role to play in this. Parents will have to devote the necessary time to explain to their children why there are people who are different—people who can't see, adults in 'strollers' like babies.

Children are natural-born researchers and philosophers. More than anything, they want to understand. The word 'why' is constantly on their lips. Often, though, their thirst for knowledge is met with embarrassment, and parental indifference nips their native inquisitiveness in the bud—to the point of forbidding them to even look at someone with a disability.

SOCRATES: Is there something one can do about this?

ALEXANDRE: It's difficult. Perhaps one shouldn't begin by forbidding to look, but rather by teaching *how* to look *differently*, with understanding. I have seen children whose behavior changed completely. Thanks to a simple explanation, they started to look at me in a more natural, friendly, authentic way. Some of my friends started out by making fun of me in public. Gradually, however, and thanks, in no small part, to the Socratic method, their initial cruelty was transformed into deep affection. What we need to overcome above all are the stereotypes and taboos that poison human relations. Fear of being authentic coupled with fear of offending cause a lot of damage.

At the Center, my friends and I always asked the newcomers to explain their disability to us; our goal was to preclude misunderstanding and create transparency. Perhaps that's why we all got along so well. There were hardly any taboos or prejudices between us, which made for a laidback atmosphere.

SOCRATES: But wasn't this a double-edged sword?

ALEXANDRE: Let's be careful not to idealize. For example, television access was fairly limited, and our cultural knowledge suffered for it. While the media can often have a negative effect, so can total lack of information. I've already told you about the difficulties I had engaging in conversation on the most mundane topics such as music, politics, or the news.

The information void we existed in subsequently gave rise, among some of us, to a kind of voyeurism—a real temptation for many of us. Some of my friends told me that they were "making up for lost time," which can be quite embarrassing when it comes to sexuality.

SOCRATES: So far, you haven't broached this subject at all.

ALEXANDRE: At the Center, the body remained hidden. It constituted a sort of taboo in and of itself—not for my companions and me, but in more general terms: institutional policy didn't foster a healthy relationship with the body. We were expected to keep it out of sight as much as possible, without being given any reasons for such secrecy. A clear and simple explanation would have gone a long way. Having to hide the body suggested that it must somehow be evil, sinful, which in turn made it an object of irresistible curiosity. This vicious circle was only the first in a series that could lead to anxiety, malaise and, eventually, to inextricable situations. What happened to one of my friends after he left the Center is a case in point: he got into the tawdriest kind of pornography. Voyeurism became for him the highest affirmation of his freedom—the ultimate form of transgression.

But if you don't mind, I'd like to go back to the dire consequences of lacking a practical sense. This seems more important to me.

As a way to unwind and reflect on all that's happened throughout the year, I like to spend summers in a monastery. In one such abbey, I met Marc, a very peculiar character. He worked in the abbey orchard and helped out in the kitchen.

His vast erudition surprised and intrigued me. Impressively knowledgeable, he could quote Sartre, Marx, Plato, Dostoevsky, and Rabelais with disconcerting ease. Over time, our conversations led to a close and constructive friendship.

Gradually, however, I began noticing certain strange behaviors about him. For instance, he would randomly mumble incoherent words in the middle of a conversation. Or he'd suddenly thrust his hands skyward and belt out incomprehensible phrases while going about some task. He called this his "ejaculatory prayers." But I wasn't overly concerned about it.

Soon I learned that the monks had taken him in for medical reasons: Marc needed a stable environment. Suffering from schizophrenia and chronic paranoia, he was incapable of living on his own. To me, labels such as these, which are all too easily attached to people, didn't really mean much. And so the adventure of our friendship happily continued. What fun we had discussing Aristotle's metaphysics, Freud's psychoanalysis, and Sartre's anthropology.

(*Socrates is silent*)

Then, one day, Marc invited me to join him for a swim in the river that skirted the abbey. While we were swimming, we embarked on a sprawling philosophical discussion. Preoccupied and exhausted, Marc got out of the water. I was about to do the same when I slipped on a rock and lost my footing. As I was feverishly flailing my arms, he simply stood there, arms akimbo, looking on impassively. I don't know by what miracle I eventually managed to pull myself out of the water. Another minute, and I would have drowned. I immediately started berating him for not coming to my aid. He claimed that he had been too lost in thought to have been able to do anything. Fortunately, the incident had ended well. On our way back, however, I continued severely reproaching him as he emitted "ejaculatory prayers" by way of expiating his misdeed.

What Marc taught me was that thinking—any kind of thinking—becomes dangerous if it loses its foothold in reality.

SOCRATES: So far you have highlighted the special bond you shared with your friends. You have explained to me that your friendship was the foundation, the solid base you could firmly stand on. I imagine that upon leaving the Center you encountered a completely different reality.

ALEXANDRE: You are touching on a sensitive issue, which I call 'affective dependency'. There is what one might call 'dependency of necessity': thus, I depend on my baker, my milkman, the cobbler who repairs my shoes, the professor who teaches me philosophy. This is what allows us to find our individual place, while keeping the interest of the collective in mind. That's how society, with its many divisions of labor, is organized.

But psychological or emotional dependency is entirely different. It generates tension. Fear of loss, fear of hurting others, fear of being rejected by a friend, or rather by the one I depend on, is a truly dangerous toxin. It instrumentalizes the other, reduces him to a means to filling a void, mitigating one's loneliness. One hangs onto, grovels toward the other only to escape oneself. "A modality of distraction," as Pascal would say. Sartre, too, addresses this problem, which I briefly touched upon earlier: he describes the other's gaze as a source of recognition and acknowledgment. As soon as I feel acknowledged by the other, I'll do anything to please him, to continue—drop by dripping drop—receiving his friendship and approbation.

SOCRATES: Let's be careful not to oversimplify!

ALEXANDRE: With the rare exception, at the Center I was constantly surrounded by friends who all got along. There was simply no physical isolation, someone was always around. When I left this environment—privileged in that way— things changed radically. I had to unlearn being in the constant company of others and come to terms with being alone.

When I say 'alone' I don't mean complete solitude. Still, the contrast remains stark. To this day, I have a hard time dealing with it. Having lived in abundance, shortages are the harder to bear. My first encounters with this new reality were certainly painful at times—though, again, profoundly formative. I have already described how I went about forming friendships quickly.

Yet I was also terribly afraid of losing my friends. My freedom was too dependent on them.

SOCRATES: When you speak of freedom, do you actually mean emotional independence?

ALEXANDRE: You are right to distinguish. I didn't choose to depend on others. No, but owing to my disability—my entire past, in fact—I felt the need for support, for friends, both male and female, all the more acutely.

Advertising, for instance, doesn't help us at all to attain true freedom and independence. It presents images of conditional happiness. Caricaturing happiness, it makes it dependent on material conditions: financial security, social status, being respected by others. It feeds our needs and stokes our desires, all the while being careful not to provide the means to ever fully satisfying them. What a cruel paradox!

When I first left the Center, my cultural knowledge was, as I've already told you, slim at best. Which may have intensified the impact of such conditioning.

I had been taught that integration was the final goal; success meant becoming like the others. But I didn't find this idea very appealing.

SOCRATES: Now I am confused. This seems like a contradiction.

ALEXANDRE: It only seems that way! I just mentioned that I wanted nothing more than to become as much like the others as possible. But, obviously, this objective could take multiple forms. Perhaps the contradiction disappears if you consider that 'being like the others' meant one thing to our caregivers and something else entirely to the child that I was.

The caregivers nurtured my need for others. They held up a conformist image of success before me—'à la Maradona'—which, even though it didn't interest me in the least, overshadowed my entire childhood. Hardwiring? Irreversible indoctrination? I don't blame anybody.

At the Center, signs of affection and encouragement from adults weren't exactly common currency, and many of my companions openly admit today to how they crave being complimented and praised. For them, the other has become an 'automatic distributor' of rewards and favors to be curried at any cost. Pity serves them as an instrument for garnering whatever praise they can get. A natural reaction: when you're hungry, you look for food; when you're thirsty, you drink; when you're starved for love, you stubbornly seek love.

SOCRATES: Let's be careful not to judge! One

ought to understand the reasons for such behavior rather than condemn it.

ALEXANDRE: All the more so since there are
those who say that education is best done 'the
hard way'. I, for one, believe the opposite: forming friendships, remedying this daunting emotional void is the only way to go. Socrates, I
think that you're touching an open wound
here ... I don't know what else to say ...

SOCRATES: Don't be afraid! Tell me more about
this emotional deprivation?

ALEXANDRE: You cannot imagine the devastat-
ing long-term effects of being wrested from
one's parents. The visceral knowledge, moreover, that we were merely *cared for*, rather than
loved, by our caregivers didn't exactly help
things either ... This emotional deficit that I
had felt since my earliest childhood hurts even
today.

SOCRATES: Doesn't understanding bring heal-
ing? Was it the same for your companions?

ALEXANDRE: More or less, but with quite distinct consequences. Some of them resorted to
all kinds of ruse to compensate for their emotional deprivations, often to dubious effect.

   I remember William. He confided to me that
he had found a way not to have to pay for public
transportation. William had an unsteady gait

and great difficulty speaking. So, whenever a conductor asked him for his ticket, he would stick out his tongue and wildly stare at him. Confused, the conductor would then leave this unusual passenger alone without requesting any payment, and William could have his cake and eat it. His travel expenses beat all competition. William's code name for this dubious strategy was "operation lizard."

SOCRATES: It is difficult not to give in to temptation …

ALEXANDRE: William claimed that he had found a way to "get back at the others." But why "get back" at anybody at all? Often, we don't know the reasons underlying someone else's actions. Using the unease generated in certain situations to one's advantage by putting on a show is a risky undertaking.

SOCRATES: Who deserves more respect: the conductor who demands payment, or the one who neglects his duty out of pity?

ALEXANDRE: That's a profoundly philosophical question. But insofar as it pertains to a concrete situation, the answer will have to remain ambiguous. After all, real-life situations are not always clear-cut. Perhaps the truth lies in the nuance. I might sound overly categorical, rigid, exacting. But that's only because I'm relating a subjective experience. I am not at all trying to saddle you with a well-constructed, meticulously thought-out theory; I am merely describing a range of impressions gathered in particular situations.

The problem of emotional deprivation was so central to us ...

SOCRATES: Was there no one, aside from your companions and your family, who could fill this void? No one who helped you to work against the "consequences" you mentioned?

ALEXANDRE: Yes, Father Morand. Religion played a major role at the Center. Many of my caregivers were religious. Some of them didn't always live by the lessons they dispensed. In philosophy, this type of inconsistency is called cognitive dissonance: the dissociation between our ideals, our will, and our actions.

There were persons of faith, however, who did help me to become who I am today. How could I reminisce about my years at the Center without mentioning Father Morand?

Every Thursday, a tall, gruff old man would show up at the chapel, wearing a frayed cassock. This was Father Morand, the chaplain. And it was this man who kindled and, little by little, nourished my passion for philosophy, which soon helped me to think through and break the bad habits instilled in me by my caregivers. Father Morand was an austere old man, cold and ordinary. As time went by, however, I discovered an extraordinary personality beneath the stern façade.

I would often go to him in the hope of demolishing his theological truths, which allowed him to exculpate a God who rendered nuns austere and condoned suffering. In the course of our regular exchanges, he became a friend, my best friend, in fact. Still, everything separated us: he was sixty years older than I and came from a completely different cultural background … Despite all that, however, we managed to establish a dialogue and build a bridge connecting our worlds.

Father Morand never preached to me. His presence and experience were enough to touch my innermost core. I am profoundly grateful to have met this old man, who, despite his failing health, endeavored to fulfill his role as the Center chaplain with fervor and joy.

His influence on me was radical; it exerted itself virtually without his doing. He transformed me, being neither a theoretician nor an eminent psychologist.

What joy it was for me to watch him pacing back and forth in his "house of variable geometry," as he referred to it. He was always available to those most in need. A mysterious man who never pontificated, Father Morand had lived through both world wars. He regaled me with many an anecdote on the subject. Here's one that will give you a sense of his character: he was sheltering a Jewish family on the run from the Gestapo in his parsonage. Seeing the dust in the air stirred up by the approaching Gestapo cars from afar, he had the presence of mind to ransack his own home. After making sure that the fugitives were securely hidden in the granary, he upended all the furniture and smashed all the dishes. When the first SS man entered, Father Morand pointed at the mess, saying: "Just look around, your colleagues have already done the job, there is no one here." The SS left and the family survived thanks to his audacious sagacity.

SOCRATES: Very clever! What a great example of a practical mind.

ALEXANDRE: What drew me to this man of God, this complex, multi-faceted individual, was his radiant personality. What an amazing human being he was! His generosity and intelligence were often misunderstood. But those who knew him well, appreciated his beneficent presence and his invaluable support.

Leading by example, he revealed the beauty of humanity to me and gave me self-confidence. I deeply cherish his legacy. Ravaged and hollowed out by disease, this man lived an extraordinary, if humble, life! It is difficult to describe the happiness Father Morand brought me. His support was beyond words, beyond deeds. His death did not cause me any pain or regret. Everything he has given me lives on in my actions, my way of thinking, my very being. Words fail in the face of this kind of friendship!

SOCRATES: Throughout your story thus far, I couldn't help noticing that, ironically, you seem to have been helped the most by those who don't seem to have been the most competent.

ALEXANDRE: I am fortunate to have met some unusual individuals along the way without whom I wouldn't have pursued my ambitions and, eventually, attended university. I don't mean erudite scholars but, simply, friends— both male and female—who, not unlike yourself, awakened a taste for higher education in me.

SOCRATES: Let's now get to the part where you are a college student. What are some of the career options you were presented with? I have a bit of a hard time envisioning this?

ALEXANDRE: At the Center, our possible careers had already been mapped out for us: manual labor in "special-needs workshops" to "pass the time." These workshops provide professional homes for the disabled who are capable of producing a variety of things at their own pace. The beguiling professional future that one caregiver had in mind for me, in particular, consisted in making cigar boxes. I would have certainly made an able 'tobacconist'!

(*Laughs*)

SOCRATES: It wasn't as funny then, was it?
ALEXANDRE: Not quite! We weren't given any personal choices! At the time, though, I didn't feel that this constricted my liberty in any way. In view of the complete lack of alternatives, I simply resigned myself to it, that's all. And why not? After all, it's not like I had a lot of options.

You can't desire what you don't know. If you've never been tipsy, you probably won't crave the pleasures of inebriation. In order to covet something, to wish to exercise this or that profession, you must first have some idea of what it might be like. And that's precisely what I didn't have. By way of caricature, let's take an example from advertising: when you see an image of chocolate, you immediately feel a craving for it. But without that image, without that stimulus, you may have never had the craving. Thus, it was only through contact with people outside the Center that the idea of attending university gradually took shape in me. Their descriptions of student life intrigued me. I, too, wanted to taste this kind of happiness; but the obstacles to this project multiplied.

SOCRATES: Birth pangs?

ALEXANDRE: Attending university was not something that came up often at the Center. In thirty years, less than ten of us managed to go. The doctors and psychologists from social services had a major, if indirect, impact on our career paths. They assessed our economic viability and advised our parents accordingly. Can you imagine these bureaucrats' surprise when I told them that I wanted to study philosophy?

SOCRATES: Easily …

ALEXANDRE: Even my IQ worked against me. Once a year, a psychologist came to the Center to measure our IQs. To me this was no more than a game, a welcome break from our school routine.

The psychologist would spend about half an hour alone with each of us in a narrow room used only on special occasions, where our reflexes were tested and where we were asked to stack boxes on top of each other (starting with the biggest), explain images, and solve math problems ... The data collected were then shuffled, producing a number that never failed to serve as a hot topic for debate during recess. My mother later told me that I had managed to garner the lowest IQ in my grade. I can't help finding this amusing.

The psychologists' conclusions—inconsistent though they may have been—were of signal importance, as they contributed to the doctors' decisions regarding our professional futures. My parents had to mount strenuous objections to be allowed to enroll me in a private school. After a lot of back and forth, I was finally accepted for half a day a week. Our perseverance had triumphed, and my success surpassed all hopes and expectations. I had soon made it to the top of the class.

SOCRATES: How do you explain this quick progress?

ALEXANDRE: No sooner had I been placed in a stimulating environment than my abilities started to rapidly flourish. I studied more than I had to so as to reach the top, adapt, integrate.

At the Center, however, the situation was completely different: I would typically work on the small typewriter that social services had eventually decided to procure for me. I took my time and didn't push myself. Fabien, sitting next to me, would be typing on his keyboard with a stick attached to his forehead, unicorn-style. He wrote ten times slower than I. Next to him was Adrien, desperately trying to trace his first name with his leaden fingers. As for me, I was bored in class and admired the beautiful winter landscape outside.

SOCRATES: You were not motivated?

ALEXANDRE: I adjusted my pace to my neighbor. When he'd finish a word, I'd do the same, only ten times faster. I'd have already spent all my energy learning to walk straight during physical therapy, climbing stairs, tying my shoelaces. Studying seemed unimportant to me, a chore, and, above all: useless. Rolling cigars was my professional horizon. Reading, writing wouldn't be of any use to me.

At my 'official' school, on the other hand, the fact that I was surrounded by students who were faster than I forced me to adapt to *their* pace; and *that* I enjoyed immensely. Later, a new purchase changed my idea of what learning was all about. Against the doctor's advice, my parents bought me a computer. What a revelation! I could now write to my friends, edit texts, which gave me the greatest of pleasures! The computer became my trusted companion. It corrected my mistakes, gave me synonyms, broadened my horizon by supplying me with information. My vocabulary mushroomed, and I experienced the most profound craving for learning! My performance at school improved, and I was allowed to enroll in trade school.

This school was an alternative that seemed to please everyone. On the one hand, it offered the perspective of a professional diploma, which met the criteria of financial profitability imposed by social services. On the other hand, it satisfied my thirst for knowledge.

Following a fairly smooth initial period of adjustment, the three years I spent there went by peacefully. I made lots of acquaintances and formed genuine friendships. In order to attend university and study philosophy, however, I still had to complete senior high school, which required advanced proficiency in Italian. Thus, I high-tailed it to Italy, where I spent an entire month catching up on a two-year curriculum.

In high school, the teachers were very understanding. They did everything they could to facilitate my work. Still, how hard it was to integrate! My classmates had already known each other for two years. Their initially warm welcome gave way to increasing withdrawal. My teachers had to devote more time to me than to the other students. The specter of jealousy started poisoning the class atmosphere.

Where did this jealousy originate? With those at the top of the class—those who deftly expatiated on tolerance, who stood up in the face of tradition and religion, who touted freedom of thought, tolerance toward the neighbor, and spoke out in favor of difference. Astonishing incoherence! But thanks to your teachings, which I had been gradually absorbing, dear Socrates, and thanks to Father Morand's counsel, I came out of this impasse with an awareness that it was ignorance above all, rather than deliberate malice, that had negatively affected the atmosphere.

SOCRATES: I begin to understand the reason for your visit.

ALEXANDRE: Practical concerns compounded the problem of integration. The computers we used made it difficult to process scientific data. Good math and physics software was scant, and so I had to dictate my science tests to my teachers, which created its own complications. Here again, the teachers had to devote extra time to my special needs, which, I imagine, stoked my classmates' ridiculous jealousy. How could I not have been deeply affected by all that? If in trade school, where the same problems had found happy solutions, integration had been a success, then in high school my survival became ever more precarious.

What a rude awakening! I had been painted a very rosy picture of my high school peers as a humane and open-minded lot. But what I actually found were internecine jealousy, rivalry, and a total lack of understanding. Still, I managed to make friends, quite good ones, in fact.

Experiencing this oppressive climate was deeply formative. It showed me that the Center, suffused as it was with the spirit of camaraderie that defined our relationships, had been an island in the middle of a vast ocean roiled by frequent and violent storms.

SOCRATES: You seem to suggest that there is something positive to be gained from every experience, even the most difficult one. Listening to you, this would seem obvious, but ...

ALEXANDRE: It's true that it takes a lot of hard work. Let me say it again: ever since I discovered philosophy, I have relentlessly endeavored to understand what is happening to me and to benefit from it.

SOCRATES: What exactly do you mean by 'understanding' and 'benefiting'?

ALEXANDRE: I was once taught that 'understanding' in the Hebrew sense means 'tasting', 'experiencing'. In Jewish culture, knowledge is distinct from a certain type of intellectualism that is the legacy of ancient Greece, which you know much better than I. For the Jews, knowing oneself means steeping oneself in one's own history in order to endow it with meaning, give it sense, gain experience.

SOCRATES: This, too, is not at all obvious!

ALEXANDRE: No, you can accumulate experiences in order to escape from reality, without considering their underlying meaning, significance, and the consequences they may have for ourselves and those around us. Thanks to reflection, however, each event can help us to construct, to choose whatever enables us to live—to choose life itself.

Let's have another look at Hebrew etymology and briefly digress on the notions of 'good' and 'bad'. In Hebrew, 'good' is used for edible mushrooms, and 'bad' for those that give us stomach cramps and are potentially lethal. Knowing oneself, then, means precisely: knowing what is good, what is good for life, rather than accumulating sterile experiences.

Many people came to work at the Center for a few days to 'gather experience'. To us, being turned into objects of study, like guinea pigs or rare clinical cases, was humiliating.

SOCRATES: Let's get back to high school—what did you learn there?

ALEXANDRE: Defeat. After trying everything both on the technical plane—in terms of remediating my inability to write—and the social plane—in terms of attempting to build a bridge between *their* world and mine—I was forced to concede that my difference was too painfully salient.

Before entering high school, I had boned up on all the curricular requirements. My future classmates had been described to me as highly knowledgeable and avid scholars. Undoubtedly, in my mind I had further embellished this picture, as I was genuinely looking forward to soon being immersed in an environment conducive to reflection and learning. My disappointment was the graver for it. The heroes I encountered were neither Rabelais nor Spinoza nor Pasteur; they were sitcom characters, Aristophanes' modern heirs. At the Center, as

I've already mentioned, we always tried to get to the heart of things together, despite our rudimentary education. We homed in on the essential. In high school, I no longer had this option. Except for the pranksters: flouting clichés, they couldn't care less about my being different and became my friends. But—all that is water under the bridge.

ALEXANDRE: Finally, the moment arrived when I entered university. I'd be living on my own for the first time, cooking my own food … This caused a lot of apprehension among those around me. My parents had to take a lot of flack and fear-driven reproach. But it had been decided: I would not live in an institution forever, no matter the cost of independence.

SOCRATES: I am dying of curiosity!

ALEXANDRE: As far as the blessings of cooking are concerned, my apprenticeship was quick. After a month of tortellini with cream sauce, I learned to fix more intricate, sophisticated dishes … But I had daunting, predatory enemies: the oven, for instance, with its gaping maw, threatened to burn my paws at every turn. Thus, to be able to extract croquettes from the oven, I devised a scheme worthy of a Napoleon: I'd open the door wearing oven mitts, prepare a plate about eight inches away, and using a spatula—golf-club style—putt the croquettes one by one, aiming to land them on my plate. At first, my progress was slow, but I still managed to score one out of ten. As I became more agile, I moved up to two, then four, five, seven, and all the way up to nine out of ten. Now, I'm impatiently awaiting the long winter evenings in order to further improve my score, which is already nothing to be ashamed of.

Each difficulty goaded me further along, became the occasion for an exciting adventure. Gradually, I attained a pretty respectable degree of autonomy. All the years of ergo-therapy were finally paying off. Still, their value paled in comparison with what I learned on my own in my studio apartment. As my mother often says: "One always manages when one is hungry." The necessity to be pushed into the world and encouraged to surpass oneself, rather than being pampered and overprotected, is crucial. But let's not exaggerate. I'll never be completely independent.

Fortunately, at the university I have found true friends of both sexes, who are happy to share their class notes with me without condescension. Working together, enriching each other, we have formed enduring bonds.

The sense of dependency and disempowerment that I felt in high school dragged me down; at the university, it has become an abundant source of energy. Fully aware that I cannot be on my own, I no longer hesitate to approach others, which in turn leads to healthy relationships. I insist on the sincerity of true friendship. Aristotle speaks of degrees of friendship. At the very top, he places the friendship between equals. Both friends enrich each other without a trace of mutual exploitation. I've had the good fortune of knowing this type of friendship, which brings me great comfort—comfort that I also enjoyed at the Center among my brothers-in-misfortune.

SOCRATES: I don't like the expression 'brothers-in-misfortune'. It somehow doesn't chime with all the joy, energy, and strength you have gone out of your way highlighting as the hallmark of your friendships at the Center.

ALEXANDRE: That's true; and I only use it for the sake of linguistic convenience. But let's get back to my current friends. In the media, we often hear that in this day and age we tend to get more and more self-centered and cut off from others, and that the number of genuine relationships is saliently dropping. Paradoxically, for me it's been the opposite. At the university, I've been spontaneously assisted by strangers on multiple occasions. Before enrolling, I had thought a lot about what I would need to be able to study like everyone else. I soon realized that relying on myself alone wouldn't cut it. Some of my fellow students have offered their support, and thanks to them I can pursue my studies virtually like a 'normal' person.

When I read for too long, I suffer from hypertension in the neck, which causes headaches. To remedy this, some of them lend me their lecture notes, while others read and record course materials for me.

SOCRATES: Doesn't being in others' debt make you bitter?

ALEXANDRE: Far from it. I find it enriching. But in order to be able to see it that way one has to overcome one's initial sense of humiliation. My incapacity to attain complete independence is a daily reminder of human greatness. At the very heart of my weakness, I can appreciate the gift of others' presence, and I in turn endeavor to make them a gift of mine, modest and fragile though it may be.

A weak person isn't necessarily a burden on others. Each of us freely disposes of his or her own weakness, and it's up to us to employ it judiciously.

SOCRATES: Weakness can become fertile in generating friendship. Is that what you have found out?

ALEXANDRE: In theory. But putting theory into practice remains a difficult task. It requires a huge effort. Wholeheartedly and completely assuming one's weakness is a constant, unremitting struggle. And victory is never guaranteed. Often, we find ourselves all alone in this endeavor, and the other's gaze can become an obstacle.

I still recall how in the beginning, as I'd leave my apartment, I'd sometimes feel a piercing pair of eyes following me from behind half-open shutters. One time, an old lady opened the shutters and called: "Go back inside, kid, you shouldn't be out on your own." These words hurt, they dampened my self-confidence for a long time to come.

But these types of reaction are singular incidents, and we shouldn't hastily generalize this complex phenomenon. Madame de Staël said: "To understand is to forgive."

SOCRATES: And you understand?

ALEXANDRE: Not quite yet. My companions and I have suffered, and continue to suffer, many wrongs that way. But we must come to terms with it, strive to understand.

It's precisely this kind of work that I've had to relentlessly perform on myself. And bit by bit, one attains a certain, fragile freedom that, though constantly under threat, is a freedom still. This apprenticeship, this knowledge was Father Morand's legacy to me: the single most important gift I've received in all my seventeen years at the Center. And this gift, which I owe to Father Morand—you, Socrates, were the one who made me desire to further explore and cultivate it. Thanks to this desire, I found the strength necessary to continue this joyful and beautiful struggle. And for this, Socrates, I sincerely thank you!

Philosophy—insofar as it battles clichés and stereotypes—has greatly helped me to oppose reason to prejudice and negative emotion, to fight unreason, fear, and cruelty. After my departure from the Center, the twofold enemy to be defeated was my own lack of self-confidence and others' incomprehension. Not only did I have to accept and assume the condition of not being normal—after all, I would never be just like everyone else, I would never be normal! But I also had to find the strength to understand others' lack of understanding in order to forgive the unforgivable—and, if possible, joyfully so.

SOCRATES: Throughout your story, you have emphasized the bonds of friendship that you shared with your companions at the Center, very strong bonds indeed. You have often spoken of your friends' generosity and depth, and of the strength you all drew from the wells of your shared weakness. Then you explained some of the methods that allowed you to adapt to the strictures of the school curriculum. Is this correct?

ALEXANDRE: Exactly!

SOCRATES: You have also described the pain that another's gaze can cause: the negative consequences of pity, mockery, misapplied good will, good conscience. You have painted a picture of the bad and the good caregiver. You have enumerated some of the difficulties you had to face after you left the Center, and the solutions you were able to come up with—in large part thanks to philosophy. But there is one last point that needs clarification.

ALEXANDRE: Did I forget something? That wouldn't be surprising.

SOCRATES: You have depicted your life at the Center at great length, as well as the process of your integration … On several occasions, you have drawn a distinction between being normal and not being normal. And you have certainly given me a definition of normality. But are you capable of and sufficiently equipped to dig deeper into this subject?

ALEXANDRE: Socrates, I think I am sufficiently prepared to satisfy your request. Actually, the distinction between 'normal' and 'not normal' has guided my entire life to this day.

It's been explained to me that normality can have two effects. It can become a stimulus for the one who feels himself excluded from it. It can trigger a desire to work on oneself and improve, thus aiming to reduce one's difference from others. But normality can also create marginality, exclusion … Many of our caregivers and psychologists talked about this.

SOCRATES: I would love to hear what they taught you about normality. What are the criteria that allow us to distinguish the person who is physically normal from the one who is not?

ALEXANDRE: Whatever deviates from the norm is by definition 'not normal'. Many features vary among the population (height, weight, et cetera). The majority of people will still fall somewhere in the middle. Thus, the more someone deviates from the norm, the less normal he will be. Your gait, your speech are much

closer to the norm than my gait and my speech
… Consequently, you are normal, and I am not.
In medicine, one typically associates the normal
person with the perfectly healthy person.

SOCRATES: This seems clear. But where would
you draw the distinction on the psychological
plane? You told me that after leaving the Center
your behavior was sometimes extreme: you expressed your feelings clumsily, you had difficulty maintaining an appropriate distance with
women, you could hardly curb an overly familiar gesture with one of your professors. Where
and how would you draw the line between 'normal' and 'not normal' in these instances?

ALEXANDRE: As I said before, behavior that we
don't consider normal deviates from the norm,
from the way the average mortal would behave.

SOCRATES: In that case, according to your definition, an exceptionally gifted person, or an extremely happy person, or even a *perfectly* normal
person would *not* be normal?

ALEXANDRE: Of course!

SOCRATES: Then you need to further specify
your definition of 'not normal'.

ALEXANDRE: Perhaps, then, 'not normal' is
whatever deviates from what one considers *ac-
ceptable* behavior.

SOCRATES: What do you mean by 'one'?

ALEXANDRE: Society at large and its norms.

SOCRATES: Didn't you tell me that you used to express your joy through cries and gestures? Would you consider this behavior *not* normal?

ALEXANDRE: It was perfectly normal behavior at the Center, and maybe that's how it is among certain peoples.

SOCRATES: This means that it is problematic to define 'not normal' exclusively according to the metric of conformity to the rules of only one society, for these rules may vary.

ALEXANDRE: One could also use the criterion of being maladjusted. That's how some define physical disability.

SOCRATES: Do you have the impression that you and your companions were maladjusted?

ALEXANDRE: No. I don't think so. But what is 'being maladjusted'?

SOCRATES: That's precisely what I want you to tell me.

ALEXANDRE: I've often heard it said that someone who is maladjusted, not normal, also feels unhappy.

SOCRATES: Is this really the case? Didn't you tell me that ever-joyful Adrien, the 'village simpleton', was your role model and your source of consolation and strength? And what about that radiant girl at the pool who had witnessed her

parents being butchered—did she feel unhappy?

ALEXANDRE: No.

SOCRATES: An exception to the rule, then? Or
was she perhaps *not* normal in a *non-normal*
way? Alexandre, where exactly does the bound-
ary lie that separates what is normal from what
is not?

ALEXANDRE: I have to admit, I don't know.

SOCRATES: Alexandre, I have an idea. And after
that, I think we'll agree on what 'normal' means:
wherever I go, whatever situation I find myself
in, everyone considers me marginal, not normal, and treats me as such; yet, I walk straight,
I obey the laws ... Prove to me, demonstrate to
me that I, for one, am completely normal!

(*Alexandre is silent*)

Born in Sierre, Switzerland, in 1975 with cerebral palsy, ALEXANDRE JOLLIEN grew up in
an institution for the severely disabled, where,
as he laconically observes, "rolling cigars" was
his "professional horizon." But then, completely
by chance, he discovered philosophy, and his
life was changed forever. Against all odds, he
succeeded in completing secondary education
and enrolled at the Université de Fribourg, thus
escaping a future staked out for him by his
caregivers. While studying abroad at Trinity
College, Dublin, he met his future wife, with
whom he has three children.

  He wrote his first book—*Éloge de la faiblesse /
In Praise of Weakness*—while still an undergraduate in philosophy in Fribourg, and has since
established himself as a profound and compelling moral thinker and spiritual teacher. Not
only is he the first and only congenitally severely disabled thinker in the history of philosophy, but he is also the first original philosopher
to have consistently reflected on what it means
to be born and live with disability not as an in-

surmountable obstacle but as a source of strength and creative energy.

A prolific writer and frequent public speaker, Alexandre Jollien has been awarded the Prix Mottart for Literature and the Prix Montyon for Ethics (both by the Académie Française). After spending three years in Seoul, South Korea, he and his family recently returned to Switzerland and currently reside in Lausanne.

*

Molecular geneticist, Buddhist monk and humanitarian MATTHIEU RICARD is the "right-hand man" of the Dalai Lama and bestselling author of *The Monk and the Philosopher: A Father and Son Discuss the Meaning of Life* (2000), *Happiness: A Guide to Developing Life's Most Important Skill* (2006), *Altruism: The Power of Compassion to Change Yourself and the World* (2015), and, most recently, *A Plea for the Animals: The Moral, Philosophical, and Evolutionary Imperative to Treat All Beings with Compassion* (2016). Matthieu Ricard's TED talk "The Habits of Happiness" has been viewed by millions.

available & forthcoming from uwsp

Designed by UWSP
Printed in the United States of America